A Primary Source History of

THE AMERICAN REVOLUTION

by Sarah Powers Webb

Consultant: Richard Bell
Associate Professor of History
University of Maryland,
College Park

CAPSTONE PRESS
a capstone imprint

Fact Finders Books are published by Capstone Press,
1710 Roe Crest Drive, North Mankato, Minnesota 56003
www.mycapstone.com

Library of Congress Cataloging-in-Publication Data
Cataloging-in-Publication Data is on file with the Library of Congress..
ISBN 978-1-4914-8487-6 (library binding)
ISBN 978-1-4914-8491-3 (paperback)
ISBN 978-1-4914-8495-1 (eBook PDF)

Editorial Credits
Brenda Haugen, editor; Sarah Bennett, designer; Wanda Winch, media researcher;
Katy LaVigne, production specialist

Photo Credits
Courtesy of Army Art Collection, U.S. Army Center of Military History, 13, 22, 26; Courtesy of the
Massachusetts Historical Society, 6; Getty Images/Hulton Archives, 5; Granger, NYC, 18; Library
of Congress: Continental Congress Broadside Collection, 28, Drafting the Documents/Declaring
Independence/June 1776, cover (top); National Archives and Records Administration, 1 (bottom),
9, 14, 15, 17, 20; Newscom: Design Pics/George Munday, 7; North Wind Picture Archives, 25;
Shutterstock: Everett Historical, 11; Superstock: Superstock, cover (bottom); Todd Andrlik, author of
Reporting the Revolutionary War (Sourcebooks, 2012), beforehistory.com, 1 (top), 8

Printed in the United States of America in North Mankato, Minnesota.
009221CGS16

TABLE OF CONTENTS

A NOTE ABOUT PRIMARY SOURCES

Primary sources are newspaper articles, photographs, speeches, or other documents that were created during an event. They are great ways to see how people spoke and felt during that time. You'll find primary sources from the time of the American Revolution throughout this book. Within the text, primary source quotations are colored *brown* and set in italic type.

REASONS FOR WAR

In the 1700s Great Britain's King George III ruled the 13 American colonies. These colonies had developed with little interference from the British government.

By 1763 Great Britain had won a war against France for control of North American land and its resources. The war left Great Britain with huge **debts** and new lands to protect. To solve its problems, the British government placed new laws on the colonies. Some of these laws required the colonists to pay taxes. Colonists felt these taxes challenged their rights. They were angry because they had no representative in British **Parliament** to vote on these laws. Some people used violence and **boycotts** to protest the taxes. Thomas Jefferson, a political leader from Virginia, said British laws were a *"deliberate … plan of reducing us to slavery."*

Other colonists felt the king knew best. **Loyalist** Thomas Hutchinson argued that *"under this constitution, for more than one hundred years, peace and order have been maintained."*

debt—something that is owed
Parliament—the national legislature of Great Britain
boycott—to stop buying something to show support for an idea or group of people
loyalist—a colonist who was loyal to Great Britain during the American Revolution

NOTHING WAS THOUGHT OF BUT THIS TAXATION,
AND THE EASIEST METHOD OF LIQUIDATION.

T-A-X

'TWAS ENOUGH TO VEX
THE SOULS OF THE MEN OF BOSTON TOWN,
TO READ THIS UNDER THE SEAL OF THE CROWN.

TAX·ON TEA· 3ᵈ per lb 1773

THEY WERE LOYAL SUBJECTS OF GEORGE THE THIRD;
SO THEY BELIEVED AND SO THEY AVERRED,
BUT THIS BRISTLING, OFFENSIVE PLACARD SET
ON THE WALLS, WAS WORSE THAN A BAYONET,

△ A cartoon shows a concerned colonist reading about the tax on tea.

The king wanted to stop the unrest. By 1769 there were nearly 4,000 British troops in Boston, a city of about 15,000 people. The prime minister of Great Britain, Lord North, said, *"We are now to establish our authority, or give it up entirely."*

In February 1770 a mob of young rioters gathered around Ebenezer Richardson, chasing him home. Richardson was an unpopular British official serving in Boston. As rioters threw stones and rocks at his house, Richardson fired a gun into the crowd. A servant named Christopher Seider was shot. He was about 11 years old.

▽ John Adams wrote in his diary about Christopher Seider's funeral.

"When I came into Town, I saw a vast Collection of People ... and found the funeral of the Child.... My Eyes never beheld such a funeral," wrote Massachusetts lawyer John Adams after seeing Seider's funeral.

Were the colonies and Great Britain bound for war? Or was there still hope they could settle their differences without more bloodshed? Only time would tell.

CRITICAL THINKING

Compare Thomas Hutchinson's point of view about taxes with Thomas Jefferson's point of view. Do you think Parliament unfairly taxed the colonists?

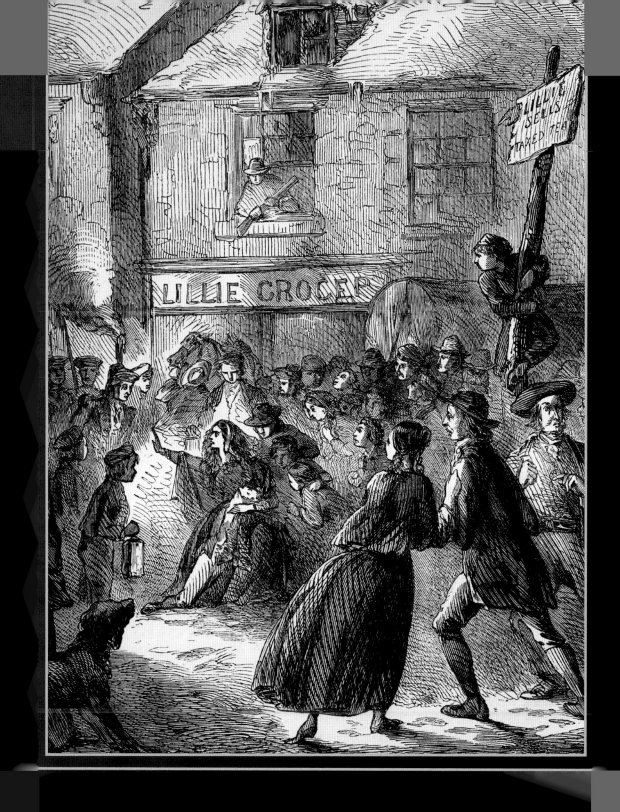

REBELLION ERUPTS

Between 1770 and 1774, Parliament forced many more taxes and laws on the colonists. Citizens continued to protest. As early as November 1774, King George III told Prime Minister North, *"blows must decide"* the fate of America.

On April 18, 1775, British General Thomas Gage sent about 700 British soldiers toward Concord, Massachusetts, to destroy colonial weapons supplies. The king also wanted to arrest colonial leaders Samuel Adams and John Hancock. As the British soldiers marched out of Boston, colonial scouts raced ahead to warn the leaders. Paul Revere, one of the scouts, said he was told *"to go to Lexington, and inform Mr. Samuel Adams, and the Hon. John Hancock Esq. that there was a number of soldiers … marching to the bottom of the common, where there was a number of boats to receive them; it was supposed that they were going to Lexington, by the way of the Cambridge River, to take them, or go to Concord, to destroy the colony stores."*

▽ A Boston newspaper gives details of the fighting in Lexington and Concord.

△ the Battle of Lexington

After Revere's warning, Adams and Hancock escaped. By the time the British arrived in Lexington about 70 **militia** members were there. British Major John Pitcairn ordered, *"Lay down your arms you ... rebels, and disperse."* No one knows who fired first, but both sides started shooting. Eighteen colonial militiamen were killed or wounded in the fighting.

The British continued their march on Concord. Once there, they destroyed weapon stores, but not much was found. **Minutemen** had already warned the town, and they had been able to hide most of the supplies. Their alarm around the countryside had also raised more militia support.

militia—a group of volunteer citizens who are organized to fight, but who are not professional soldiers
Minutemen—colonists who were ready and willing to

While the British searched Concord, a fire started at the blacksmith shop and courthouse. Militiamen became worried the whole town might burn down. In an effort to save the town, they confronted British soldiers in an exchange of gunfire. The fighting surprised the British troops so much, they decided to retreat to Boston. As the British fled, militiamen shot at them from behind trees, bushes, and walls. *"We were fired at from all quarters, but particularly from the houses on the roadside, and the Adjacent Stone walls,"* a British soldier said later.

About 270 British soldiers were killed, wounded, or missing. Only about 95 American militia were dead or missing. The *Salem Gazette* reported on the *"Bloody Butchery"* by the British troops. *"Last Wednesday, the nineteenth of April, the troops of his Britannic Majesty commenced hostilities upon the people of this province … with … cruelty not less brutal than what our ... Ancestors received from the vilest savages of the wilderness."* The battles of the American Revolution had begun.

△ Militiamen turned back the British at Concord.

CRITICAL THINKING

Compare the number of British soldiers and American militia killed and wounded in the battles of Lexington and Concord. Then read the *Salem Gazette* newspaper description of the event. Do you agree with this description? Why or why not?

REVOLUTION

After the battles of Lexington and Concord, **patriot** militia gathered at Breed's Hill, across the Charles River from Boston. *"Several Thousand are now Assembled about this Town Threatning an Attack"* and *"we are very busy in making Preparations to oppose them,"* wrote British General Thomas Gage. Patriot soldiers had been busy building fences, trenches, and dirt walls to protect their position.

British soldiers attacked the Patriot's defenses on Breed's Hill on June 17. British General John Burgoyne thought it would be easy for professional British soldiers to defeat the *"untrained rabble."*

Both sides fought bitterly, sometimes hand to hand. A British soldier complained that Patriots hid *"behind trees etc till an opportunity presents itself of taking a shot"* then *"they immediately retreat. What an unfair method of carrying on a war!"* After three charges up the hill, the British eventually won the battle. But they suffered great losses. Of their 2,200 soldiers, more than 1,000 were dead or wounded. More than 400 patriots were killed or wounded. Though most of the fighting took place on Breed's Hill, the fight became known as the Battle of Bunker Hill, named for a nearby hill.

patriot—a person who sided with the colonies during the American Revolution

△ British soldiers clashed with colonists on Breed's Hill.

In November 1775 Lord Dunmore, British royal governor of Virginia, offered slaves and bonded servants freedom in exchange for fighting for the British. About 5,000 African-Americans—both freemen and slaves—fought for the patriot cause. As many as 30,000 may have helped the British cause. Some slaves hoped that by fighting they would win their freedom.

In May and June 1775, representatives from all 13 colonies held a series of meetings known as the Second Continental Congress. During these sessions, Congress created the Continental Army under Commander in Chief George Washington. *"As the Congress desire it, I will enter upon the momentous duty, and exert every power I possess in their service, and for support of the glorious cause,"* Washington said.

On July 3, 1775, Washington formally took over command of the new Continental Army in Cambridge, Massachusetts. He found a ragtag army of volunteers. Many were farmers with little training and few supplies. He described the army as *"a mixed multitude of people under very little discipline, order or government."*

▽ Volunteers were sought for the colonial army.

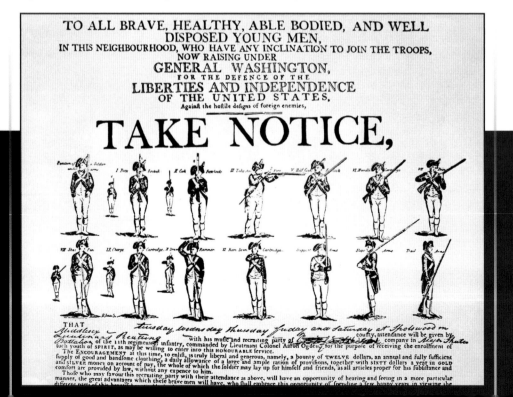

Washington knew he needed more weapons to defeat the British. He sent Colonel Henry Knox to retrieve cannons at Fort Ticonderoga. Vermont militia had recently captured the fort from British soldiers. Two months after being sent to Ticonderoga, Knox returned to Cambridge with over 50 **artillery** pieces.

The British were trapped by land, but they eventually retreated by sea. However, they were not done fighting. On August 23, 1775, King George III, declared the colonies to be in open **rebellion**.

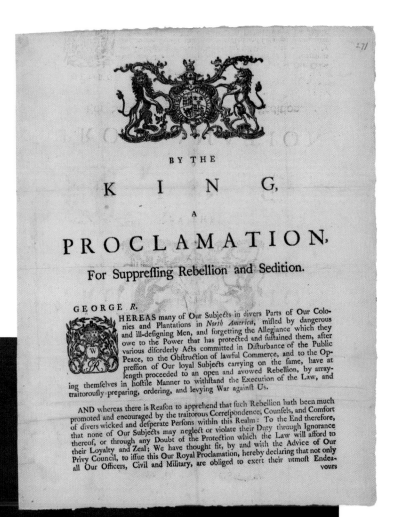

By THE

K I N G,

A

PROCLAMATION,

For Suppressing Rebellion and Sedition.

◁ Printings of the king's proclamation were sent throughout the colonies.

artillery—cannons and other large guns designed to strike an enemy at a distance
rebellion—an armed revolt against a government

15

EARLY BATTLES

Washington did not know where the British would attack next, but he had a good guess. In April 1776 Washington marched his 19,000 soldiers from Boston to Long Island to defend New York City. He did not want to lose a key city to the British. Its port was in a more central location from which the British could attack the north, the middle, or the southern colonies.

Washington had guessed correctly. In the summer of 1776, British General Sir William Howe created a New York headquarters on Staten Island. The British had 32,000 troops, 10,000 sailors, 400 ships, and 1,200 cannons.

On August 22, 1776, the British attacked. Over four days the patriots battled the British. By the afternoon of August 27, Howe had cornered the patriots on Long Island against the East River. The British Navy guarded the river. Howe outsmarted Washington in their first big battle. John Adams wrote to his wife, Abigail, *"in general, our Generals were out generalled on Long Island…."*

Howe delayed further attack and the next day dug trenches around Washington's troops. A large storm also hit the area. During the delay, Washington decided to retreat. He saw that his position could not be held. During the night of August 29 and into the morning of the August 30, Washington ferried his troops across the river.

But time ran out. Not all the troops were across the river by sunrise. In a stroke of luck, a heavy fog hit the area. It allowed the remaining soldiers to ferry across the river. By the time the British discovered what Washington was doing, it was too late. The Continental Army had escaped.

By September 15 the British had control of New York City. On September 16 the Continental Army held their ground at the Battle of Harlem Heights. Then on October 28, they again met the British in a bitter battle in White Plains, New York. From there Washington withdrew to New Jersey with his troops, losing forts to the British along the way. Finally, in early December, the British chased the patriots from Trenton, New Jersey, across the Delaware River into Pennsylvania.

◁ Washington directed the retreat from Long Island.

Washington realized his untrained army would not be able to defeat the skilled British soldiers head on. *"When the fate of America may be at stake ... when the Wisdom of cooler moments and experienced Men have decided that we should **protract** the War if Possible; I cannot think it safe or wise to adopt a different System,"* Washington wrote.

From the beginning of the war, the British dominated the seas. The patriots started the war with no navy. Congress created a Continental Navy in October 1775. The Continental Navy always had fewer ships than the British Royal Navy. To help, Americans used **privateers**. Privateers captured or destroyed nearly 600 British ships during the American Revolution.

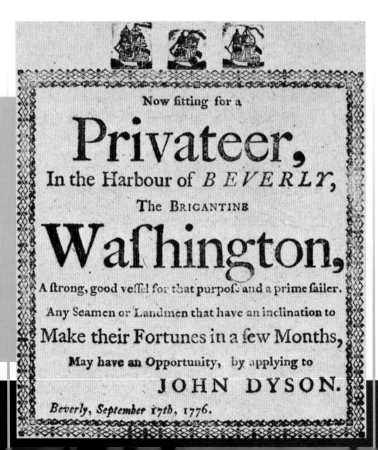

Now fitting for a

Privateer,

In the Harbour of *BEVERLY*,

The BRIGANTINE

Wafhington,

A ftrong, good veffel for that purpofe and a prime failer.

Any Seamen or Landmen that have an inclination to

Make their Fortunes in a few Months,

May have an Opportunity, by applying to

JOHN DYSON.

Beverly, September 17th, 1776.

An ad urged men to sign up for service on a privateer in Beverly Harbor, Massachusetts

In the winter of 1776 the patriots camped near Bristol, Pennsylvania. Across the Delaware River lay **Hessian**-occupied Trenton, New Jersey. Howe's army was in a position to conquer the New Jersey colony and strike Philadelphia, the Americans' capital city. The British offered New Jersey citizens a chance to surrender in exchange for a pardon from the king. Nearly 3,000 citizens jumped at the chance. George Washington was disgusted. *"Instead of turning out to defend the country and offering aid to our Army, they are making their submissions as fast as they can,"* Washington said.

Usually armies did not fight during the winter. It was too hard to move troops and supplies during the cold winter months. But Washington was desperate. His soldiers had few supplies, many had no shoes, and there was little food. Also, as many as half of his 3,000 soldiers would complete their **enlistment** by the end of the year. Most planned to go home. Washington knew he had to act. *"That Christmas-day at night, one hour before day, is the time fixed upon for our attempt on Trenton ... necessity, dire necessity will, nay must, justify any attempt,"* Washington wrote to Colonel Joseph Reed.

protract—to draw out or lengthen in time; prolong
privateer—a person who owns a ship licensed to attack and steal from other ships
Hessian—a German soldier hired by the British
enlist—to voluntarily join a branch of the military

△ Soldiers tried to avoid the ice as they crossed the Delaware with George Washington.

On the night of December 25, 1776, Washington crossed the Delaware River with 2,700 men. The river was full of ice, so the crossing went slowly and took longer than expected. After landing in the early hours of December 26, Washington's troops marched 9 miles (14.5 kilometers) to Trenton, New Jersey. Some soldiers were still barefoot.

The surprise attack caught the Hessians off guard. Many had been celebrating Christmas and were sleeping. In the Battle of Trenton, the patriots captured, killed, or wounded nearly 1,100 soldiers. Washington proudly wrote about his troops in a letter to fellow patriot John Hancock. *"Their Behaviour upon this Occasion, reflects the highest honor … the difficulty of passing the River in a very severe Night, and their March thro' a violent Storm of Snow and Hail did not in the least abate their Ardour,"* Washington wrote.

The Continental Army went on to win a battle at Princeton, New Jersey, on January 3, 1777. Washington became a national hero. Many New Jersey citizens again switched sides to support the patriot cause.

But patriot leaders knew they would not likely win the war without more help. On October 27, 1776, Benjamin Franklin, a famous scientist and political leader, left for France. His goal was to convince the French to help the patriots fight the war. France was already secretly giving the Americans money and military supplies. But the patriots hoped for more help in the form of French troops and its navy.

In 1760 Benjamin Franklin believed the colonies should support the king. In 1763 Franklin's son, William, became the royal governor of New Jersey. By 1775 Franklin had changed his mind and supported the patriot cause. His son remained a loyalist. Franklin and his son never reconciled.

THE TIDE TURNS

By 1777 British General John Burgoyne presented a bold plan to the king. The general believed that by cutting off New England from the other colonies, the British could win the war. His plan included troops marching south from Canada toward Albany, New York. He planned to conquer towns along the Hudson River. This would prevent colonists from getting supplies up the river as well as across it to either side. On June 17 Burgoyne marched south from Canada with more than 8,000 troops.

If the march had gone according to plan, it might have worked. But Burgoyne's trip was time-consuming. For one thing, he over-packed. His personal baggage took up nearly 30 carts that stretched for nearly 3 miles (4.8 km). Thick forests and river crossings slowed travel progress. Patriot militia also tried to prevent British progress as much as possible by blocking the path. William Digby, a British soldier among Burgoyne's troops, said at one point, *"we marched … but could only proceed about 6 miles, the road being broke up by the enemy and large trees felled across it, taking up a long time to remove them for our 6 pounders, which were the heavyest guns with us."*

Colonial soldiers waited in the woods to attack General Burgoyne and his troops.

Patriot General Horatio Gates and almost 7,000 soldiers waited at Bemis Heights just south of Saratoga, New York. The two sides fought about 1 mile (1.6 km) north of Bemis Heights on September 19. The British held their ground that day, but about 550 British soldiers were killed or wounded.

Burgoyne thought more help would come from New York City. He waited nearly three weeks, but no more troops ever came. This gave the patriots time to gather more forces. About 6,800 British troops faced more than 10,000 patriots under General Gates on October 7. But during the battle, it was patriot leader Benedict Arnold who saved the day. His leadership helped rally the American troops under heavy fire. By the end of the day, the patriots controlled the battlefield and forced the British to retreat. Burgoyne surrendered October 17.

Many historians consider this battle to be a turning point in the war. Because of this victory, by February 1778 the French agreed to a military **alliance**.

alliance—an agreement between nations

After the defeat at Saratoga, the British shifted strategy. They adopted a more ruthless plan to recruit rebel leaders, as well as using their navy to bombard America's southern ports. They hoped to rally the support of slaves, American Indians, and loyalists in the southern colonies.

On December 28, 1778, the British took Savannah, Georgia, an important port city. British troops met only minor patriot resistance. *"The Rebels were so intimidated that they fled ... leaving us in quick Possession of the Town,"* a British soldier wrote to his wife. Augusta, Georgia, soon fell, and the British set their sights on South Carolina.

Beginning in April 1780, British General Sir Henry Clinton began bombarding Charleston, South Carolina. On May 12, 1780, the patriot militia surrendered nearly 5,500 troops. It was the worst patriot loss of the war. British soldiers raided southern plantations as they went. Janet Schaw, a Scottish woman visiting her brother, wrote of the British, *"At present the martial law stands thus: An officer or committeeman enters a plantation with his posse. The alternative is proposed. Agree to join us and your persons and properties are safe ... if you refuse, we are directly to cut up your corn, shoot your pigs, burn your houses, seize your Negroes and perhaps tar and feather yourself."* After these British successes, Clinton left Lord Charles Cornwallis in charge of the southern British forces.

the Battle of King's Mountain ▷

Patriot General Gates rushed into South Carolina to stop the British advance. His troops suffered a huge defeat at Camden, South Carolina, on August 16, 1780. About 900 patriots were dead or wounded, and another 1,000 surrendered. The British lost more than 300 men. A patriot soldier at the battle wrote, *"a great majority of the militia, (at least two-thirds of the army) fled without firing a shot."* Not only did the patriots suffer a great loss, but Gates destroyed his military career.

Meanwhile, Cornwallis was eager to take on the patriots. His main forces reached Charlotte, North Carolina. But on October 7 at the Battle of King's Mountain, South Carolina, the patriots defeated one band of his loyalist militia. This defeat forced Cornwallis again to retreat farther south.

General Washington had to act to stop the British advance. He named Nathanael Greene commander of the southern patriot army. Greene's plan was to draw the British far away from their supply ships on the coast to wear them down. Greene wrote to General Washington about the British commander, *"Lord Cornwallis will not give up this Country without being soundly beaten … but I am in hopes by little and little to reduce him in time."* Cornwallis chased Greene's troops in a series of battles throughout North Carolina and South Carolina in early 1781. Greene said, *"We can run in any direction, as long as it is away."*

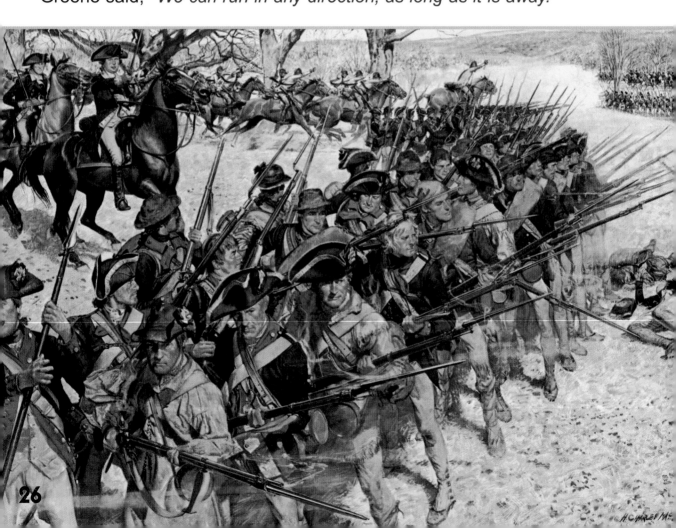

Cornwallis became determined to hunt Greene's army down. He followed Greene's troops to Guilford Courthouse, North Carolina. By the end of the day on March 15, 1781, British troops won the battlefield, but at a high cost. More than one-fourth of British troops—about 500 men—were killed or wounded. After the battle Greene wrote, *"The battle was long … and bloody. We were obligd to give up the ground, and lost our Artillery. But the enemy have been so soundly beaten, that they dare not move towards us...."*

In order to follow Greene so far inland, Cornwallis had been forced to cut ties with his supply ships on the coast. His troops were in bad shape. They withdrew to Wilmington, North Carolina, to resupply and regroup. Cornwallis planned to attack the patriots in Virginia. He wanted General Clinton in New York to send more forces to Virginia. Clinton refused. This disagreement allowed Americans time to increase their forces in Virginia.

◁ General Nathanael Greene commanded his troops at Guilford Courthouse.

British officers found a colonial leader who was willing to trade sides. In 1779 Benedict Arnold began secretly planning with General Clinton to turn over West Point, New York, a major military fort. Arnold was a proud leader who felt he never got the respect or money he deserved fighting for the patriots. His plan to turn over West Point was discovered, but Arnold escaped and later became a British general. Arnold justified his actions in part by hinting that Americans could not fight for independence and yet still support slavery. He claimed Americans hold a false *"affection for the liberties of mankind, while"* they keep *"her Native Sons in … Chains."*

LIBERTY

In August 1781 Washington learned that the French navy would sail 29 ships and 3,000 troops to the Chesapeake Bay. Washington realized he might be able to defeat Cornwallis' British forces in Virginia. On August 19 Washington and French Commander Comte de Rochambeau marched from New York to Virginia. They left a small force near New York to fool British general Clinton. By September 5, 1781, a French fleet had sailed to Virginia and battled a small fleet of British ships just off the Cheseapeake Bay. The damaged British ships retreated to New York City. The French fleet now controlled the entrance to the Chesapeake Bay.

By September the British army in Yorktown, Virginia, included about 9,000 troops supported by several thousand escaped slaves. While Washington and Rochambeau marched toward Virginia, French Major General Marquis de Lafayette's troops helped Greene's soldiers keep Cornwallis pinned at Yorktown.

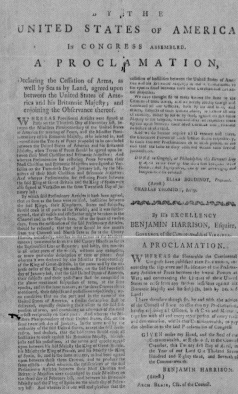

The Continental Congress announced the end of the American Revolution.

By October nearly 17,000 patriot and French soldiers blocked Cornwallis' escape. French ships prevented him from getting more supplies and aid by sea. Cornwallis could not retreat, and he could not win. He surrendered to Washington on October 19. Cornwallis wrote to Clinton, *"Sir ... I have been forced to give up ... and to surrender the troops under my command ... as prisoners of war to the combined forces of America and France."* The Battle of Yorktown ended the major fighting of the American Revolution.

In March 1782 Benjamin Franklin began peace talks with Great Britain in France. Patriot leaders John Adams, John Jay, and Henry Laurens later joined Franklin as part of the peace team. Franklin's grandson, William Temple Franklin, served as the group's secretary. After more than a year of meetings, representatives from Great Britain, France, and the United States signed the Treaty of Paris on September 3, 1783. Two days later John Adams wrote Congress that *"On Wednesday, the 3d day of this month, the American ministers met the British minister at his lodgings at the Hôtel de York, and signed, sealed, and delivered the definitive treaty of peace between the United States of America and the King of Great Britain."*

The Treaty of Paris formally ended the war. The Americans had won their independence from Great Britain.

A painting by Benjamin West of the Treaty of Paris signing includes the American representatives but not the British. The British chose not to sit for a painting that showed their defeat. To this day the painting is unfinished.

SELECTED BIBLIOGRAPHY

"A Look at the Birth of the Continental Navy." America's Navy. 21 Oct. 2009. www.navy.mil/submit/display.asp?story_id=49113

Haven, Kendall F. *Voices of the American Revolution: Stories of Men, Women, and Children Who Forged Our Nation.* Englewood, Colo.: Libraries Unlimited, 2000.

Isaacson, Walter. *Benjamin Franklin: An American Life.* New York: Simon & Schuster, 2003.

Memorial Hall Museum Online. www.memorialhall.mass.edu/collection/itempage.jsp?itemid=16201&img=0&level=advanced&transcription=1

Middlekauff, Robert. *The Glorious Cause: The American Revolution, 1763–1789.* New York: Oxford University Press, 2005.

Nash, Gary B. *The Unknown American Revolution: The Unruly Birth of Democracy and the Struggle to Create America.* New York: Viking, 2005.

Rhodenhamel, John, ed. *The American Revolution: Writings from the War of Independence.* New York: Library of America, 2001.

"The Declaration of Independence." The Charters of Freedom. www.archives.gov/exhibits/charters/declaration_transcript.html

"The Revolutionary War 1775–1783." Naval History and Heritage Command. www.history.navy.mil/browse-by-topic/heritage/banners/battle-streamers/the-revolutionary-war-1775-1783.html

Walmsley, Andrew S. *Thomas Hutchinson and the Origins of the American Revolution.* New York: New York University Press, 1999.

Wood, Gordon S. *Revolutionary Characters: What Made the Founders Different.* New York: Penguin Books, 2006.

Wood, W.J. *Battles of the Revolutionary War, 1775–1781.* New York: Da Capo Press, 1995.

GLOSSARY

alliance (uh-LYE-uhnts)—an agreement between nations or groups of people to work together

artillery (ar-TI-luhr-ee)—cannons and other large guns designed to strike an enemy at a distance

boycott (BOY-kot)—to stop buying something to show support for an idea or group of people

debt (DET)—something that is owed

enlist (en-LIST)—to voluntarily join a branch of the military

Hessian (HEH-shuhn)—a German soldier hired by the British

loyalist (LOI-uh-list)—a colonist who was loyal to Great Britain during the American Revolution

militia (muh-LISH-uh)—a group of volunteer citizens who are organized to fight, but who are not professional soldiers

Minutemen (MIH-nuht-men)—colonists who were ready and willing to fight at a moment's notice

Parliament (PAHR-luh-muhnt)—the national legislature of Great Britain

patriot (PAY-tree-uht)—a person who sided with the colonies during the American Revolution

privateer (prye-vuh-TEER)—a person who owns a ship licensed to attack and steal from other ships

protract (proh-TRAKT)—to draw out or lengthen in time; prolong

rebellion (ri-BEL-yuhn)—an armed revolt against a government

INTERNET SITES

FactHound offers a safe, fun way to find Internet sites related to this book. All of the sites on FactHound have been researched by our staff.

Here's all you do:

Visit *www.facthound.com*

Type in this code: 9781491484876

 Check out projects, games and lots more at **www.capstonekids.com**

INDEX